Fabric Painting
with Cindy Walter

- A Beginner's Guide
- 11 Techniques
- From Colorwashes to Painted Quilts

C&T PUBLISHING

Text copyright © 2011 by Cindy Walter

Photography and Artwork copyright © 2011 by
C&T Publishing, Inc.

Publisher: Amy Marson

Creative Director: Gailen Runge

Acquisitions Editor: Susanne Woods

Editor: Lynn Koolish

Technical Editor: Ann Haley

Cover Designer: Kristen Yenche

Book Designer: Christina D. Jarumay

Production Coordinator: Zinnia Heinzmann

Production Editor: Alice Mace Nakanishi

Illustrator: Kirstie L. Pettersen

Photography by Christina Carty-Francis and Diane Pedersen
of C&T Publishing, Inc., unless otherwise noted

Published by C&T Publishing, Inc., P.O. Box 1456,
Lafayette, CA 94549

Library of Congress Cataloging-in-Publication Data

Walter, Cindy.
 Fabric painting with Cindy Walter : a beginner's guide :
11 techniques, from colorwashes to painted quilts /
Cindy Walter.
   p. cm.
 ISBN 978-1-60705-217-3
 1. Textile painting. I. Title.
 TT851.W363 2011
 746.9'2--dc22
                                          2010054235

10 9 8 7 6 5 4 3 2 1

Contents

DEDICATION

To my darling husband, Michael A. Lilly

ACKNOWLEDGMENTS

My first exposure to out-of-this-world beautiful fabric was at a quilt show, where I found pieces of fabric hand painted by Mickey Lawler. I treasured the pieces that I bought, and Mickey continues to be my painting hero. For anyone wanting to paint stormy, bold landscape fabrics, I strongly recommend Mickey Lawler's Skydyes (C&T Publishing, available as an ebook; see Resources, page 78) and Mickey Lawler's SkyQuilts (C&T Publishing).

My next exposure to hand-painted fabric was soft, dreamy pieces painted by Jennifer Priestley. Years later, in 2002, Jennifer and I coauthored my first book that included painting, The Basic Guide to Dyeing and Painting Fabrics (Krause Publications, out of print).

My painting experience started simply by experimenting. But over the years, I became more knowledgeable after reading and researching information from paint and brush manufacturers. I thank these companies for generously sharing their vast knowledge. I especially appreciate the staff and management of Jacquard Products, Liquitex Artist Materials, and FM Brush Company, Inc.

I thank the students who have taken my painting workshops over the past ten years. I often learn from their creativity and spontaneity. Their love and appreciation of my workshops helped inspire me to write this book.

Most important, I thank my friends and family, who endured endless months of me being "too busy" to participate in their normal lives. And a very special thank you to my dear husband, Michael, and son, Alex, who gave me their undying support and love during this process.

Introduction

This beautiful piece of fabric was painted with a colorwash (page 22) and then rubbed with Shiva Paintstiks (page 62). It was in my reject pile until I added the paintstick rubbing.

Welcome to the world of painting on fabric. This book will show you that using paints on fabric is not only easy but also fun and often addictive. You cannot make a mistake. And unlike with other colorants, there are no complicated recipes to follow.

The secret lies in the method of application. I encourage you to approach fabric painting with a touch of whimsy. Don't be afraid to play and experiment. I can't tell you how many times in my workshops I've heard the refrain, "I'm not creative."

If you learn just one thing from me, I hope it is to relax! Don't worry about the results; just play and enjoy the process.

Results will vary depending on the brand of paint, the amount of water or medium added, and even the humidity in the air. Keep a log of your experiments. Save any "not so beautiful" pieces of fabric to play with later. Some of my favorite pieces are ones that I transformed after resurrecting them from my reject pile.

The first chapters in this book teach basic information to help you understand paints, supplies, and how to set up your work space. The Techniques and Projects section (pages 17–64) teaches application methods. Read through the opening chapters; then pick a project or technique most interesting to you. If you have never used paints on cloth, I suggest you experiment with the Dry or Wet? technique (pages 18–21) before starting a project, as that exercise is designed to give you a secure feeling about painting on fabric.

Paints

Paints and Dyes

Most fabric colorants fall into the category of paints or dyes. In this book, we will be using acrylic paints. People tend to confuse color mediums because the words are interchangeable when used as a verb. For instance, you can paint with a dye or dye with a paint. But when referring to these mediums as nouns, they are not the same substance. They have distinctive differences and are not even manufactured from the same colorants.

Although I am partial to paints, I use dyes when I need to color large amounts of fabric or want a very bold color. Knowing the distinguishing characteristics between paints and dyes will help you decide which type of product to use.

Another popular colorant is ink. This term is used loosely; depending on the manufacturer, ink can be either an acrylic paint or a dye. I often use fabric ink pens, such as Tee Juice Fabric Markers (by Jacquard) or Fabrico Dual Markers (by Tsukineko), when drawing details, and I have found that the Liquitex Acrylic Inks! (by Liquitex Artist Materials) are great for colorwashes.

PAINTS VERSUS DYES

ACRYLIC PAINTS

- Water based and clean up with water
- For use on all fabrics or fibers
- Easy to use, with no complicated recipes
- Usually set or cure over time; to speed up the process, simply press with a hot iron
- Opaque and metallic paints work beautifully on dark fabric.
- The painted fabric surface may look flat to the eye.
- Time consuming when coloring large quantities

DYES

- Dyed fabric colors are translucent, clear, and brilliant.
- Possible to vat dye large quantities of fabric at one time
- Fiber sensitive; match dye type to fabric type
- Time consuming to set
- Often use toxic mordants or complicated recipes
- Not useful with dark fabrics

Paints and Their Uses

I recommend textile paints or high-quality, artist-grade acrylic paints. If you use paints designed for surfaces such as plastic or wood, the paint may crack after it is dry on the fabric, or it may have a stiff or rubbery texture. Even adding a fabric medium to these paints won't always leave fabric with a soft hand. I've included a list of recommended paints for each project to ensure your success.

Acrylic paints appropriate for fabrics are manufactured with binders that have consistencies that vary from thin to thick. Various characteristics are achieved by suspending the pigments in the different bases or binders. Paints are considered *transparent, translucent, semitransparent, semiopaque,* and *opaque,* depending on how they are made and what they are made from.

If the paint is opaque, it will cover whatever is underneath it; if it is transparent, the colors and shapes underneath will show through. Translucent, semitransparent, and semiopaque are somewhere in between.

Thin paint allows your paint colors to bleed together. Thick paint can be applied so your colors won't bleed. Thick paint can also be thinned with water or mediums to make it a thin consistency.

When deciding which type of paint to use, you must first consider the painting technique. For instance, if you want to create a colorwash, the paint should be thin. If you want to stamp or directly paint a picture, the paint must be thick. If you are working on dark fabric or if it is important that the paint completely cover what you are painting on, use an opaque paint. If you definitely want what's underneath the paint to show through, use a transparent paint. You should also consider how the fabric will be used: If you are making a wall quilt, the final hand of the fabric is less important than if you are painting a silk scarf. The recommended type of paint is listed in the supply list for each project.

Buying paints can be confusing. Some paints have catchy names that do not always state their style or consistency; others state exactly what they are. Read the label first (or the product description if you are buying online).

- Make sure the product is acrylic or water based.

- Look for the words *soft body, light body, fluid, flowable,* or *free-flowing.*

- Look at the label to see whether the paint is transparent, translucent, semitransparent, semiopaque, or opaque.

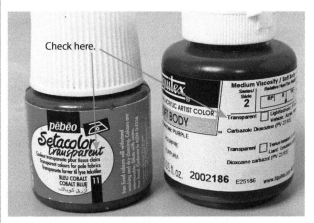

Check paint bottle labels for transparency indications.

With a few brands, the easiest way to determine the style is simply to shake the bottle. If the paint is thin, you can use it for techniques such as Colorwashes (page 22). If the paint is thick, you can use it for techniques that require a thicker paint, such as Stamping (page 56) or Stenciling (page 59), or you can thin the paint.

All the techniques and projects in this book are designed for water-based acrylic products, with the exception of the few techniques (see Stenciling, page 59; Rubbings, page 62) that use oil-based Shiva Paintstiks.

❖ CARING FOR YOUR PAINT

Paints are sterile and can last for years if you avoid contamination. Never dip your brush into the paint bottle. Never pour water or medium into the bottle unless you plan to use the entire bottle that day. Pour less paint than you need, as it can dry up if your work is interrupted. Never pour paint back into the bottle. Always replace the lid on the paint bottle immediately after pouring.

TRANSPARENT PAINT

With transparent paint, you can see through each layer that you paint. Sometimes it has the consistency of milk; sometimes it is thicker. When thin, the paint will bleed and spread like a dye. It is suitable for all fabric types and perfect for popular techniques such as colorwashing, sun printing, and salting. However, because you have little control over where thin paint flows, it is not usually used in techniques that require a thicker paint.

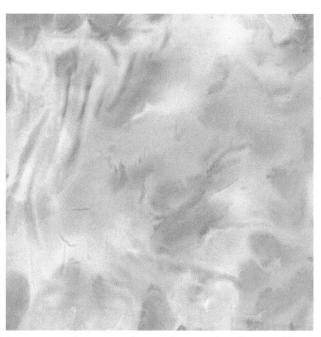

Transparent paints are translucent—for example, yellow over blue creates green. These paints create beautiful colorwashes and are used when you simply want to color fabric.

Some transparent paints require dilution with water. Dilution recommendations are listed on most bottles—for example, 1 part water to 4 parts paint or 1 part water to 1 part paint. For varying results, you can dilute the paint more than the recommended amount; however, too much water will prevent the color particles from having proper suspension, thus causing washed-out colors and dark-edged halo effects on drying. A fabric medium or colorless extender is also a good choice for thinning the paint, because it allows the paint to flow without breaking down its binder (see Mediums, page 10).

Recommended transparent products include Liquitex Acrylic Ink!, Liquitex Soft Body Acrylic (check back of bottle for level of transparency; dilute for a thin, flowable consistency), Jacquard Dye-na-Flow, Pebeo Setasilk, and Pebeo Setacolor Transparent (dilute to a thin, flowable consistency).

OPAQUE PAINT

With opaque paint, you can't see through a layer of paint. It is suitable for all fabric types and perfect when you need to control where the paint flows for direct painting techniques, such as in stamping, stenciling, monoprinting, and painting a picture. The thickness of the paint can alter the fabric's feel or hand.

Opaque or semiopaque paints are a good value because in addition to using them for opaque techniques, you can dilute them with water or fabric medium and use them for several of the transparent paint techniques. However, they are not suitable for sun printing or salting.

Recommended opaque products include Liquitex Soft Body Acrylic, Jacquard Neopaque, Jacquard Textile Colors, and Pebeo Setacolor and Setacolor Opaque.

IRIDESCENT OR METALLIC PAINTS

These paints fall into the opaque category. They have metal particles that reflect light suspended in an opaque base. They can be used in many ways: directly from the bottle as a thick paint, diluted up to 1 part paint to 1 part water for a thin consistency, or added to any other type of paint.

Recommended metallic products include Liquitex Soft Body Acrylic Iridescent, Liquitex Acrylic Ink! Iridescent, Jacquard Lumiere, and Pebeo Setacolor Pearl.

Bamboo, by Cindy Walter, 28" × 35", 2007

When Fairfield Processing first released its bamboo batting in 2007, company president Jason Young asked me to make a quilt using bamboo batting. It was quite an honor, and I greatly enjoyed the process. As you can see, I designed this quilt to reflect bamboo inside and out! For this style of direct painting, I used thick, opaque paints to paint the bamboo picture over a background created with free-flowing transparent paints

Metallic Abstract, by Cindy Walter, 16" × 21", 2008

The abstract lines in this quilt were drawn with a pencil before I painted directly with thick, metallic paints.

Mediums

Adding a medium will change a paint's behavior. In particular, mediums extend the drying time so you can work longer with the paint. They also make the paint more spreadable. Mediums can also be used to seal, adhere, or coat surfaces, or to create textures. My favorites are Liquitex Fabric Medium, Jacquard Colorless Extender, and Liquitex Matte Gel Medium.

Fabric mediums give acrylic paint a softer hand once dry on the fabric. You do not need to use a fabric medium with textile paints, though using one does have advantages. For example, it changes the volume of the paint, making it more spreadable and translucent, and it extends the working time before the paint dries.

I enjoy working with matte gel because it greatly extends the paint's drying time. This gives me time to spread or blend colors, especially if I paint the gel onto fabric as a base. When used as a topcoat, it is a perfect medium for sealing a project from water or protecting it from light. However, although this product has strong attributes and is worth using, it does give fabric a thicker, stiffer feeling.

Setting Paint

Several brands of acrylic paints recommend heat setting with an iron. Read and follow the manufacturer's directions.

Most textile paints don't need to be heat set. Some set immediately; others take a few weeks before the paint is permanent, washable, and colorfast. However, heat setting with an iron will speed the setting process. I suggest letting the paint cure for a few days and then ironing with a hot iron before using the fabric in a project.

Color

A basic knowledge of color will help you decide which paint colors to buy and what to expect when you mix or blend paint colors. The following is a summary of the most commonly used color theory, called the primary color theory.

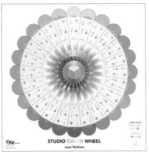

Color tools (by C&T Publishing) make understanding color theory easy.

In the primary color theory, there are three primary colors: yellow, blue, and red. Any two primary colors mixed together make a secondary: yellow + blue = green, blue + red = purple, red + yellow = orange. A primary and the adjoining secondary make a tertiary, or intermediate, color, such as teal.

Mixing colors always requires more paint of the lighter hue. The exact mixture varies by brand of paint. With Liquitex Soft Body Acrylics, for example, mix about 4 parts yellow to 1 part blue to get green. Start with the lightest hue in your bowl and slowly, sparingly add the darker color until you have the desired result.

When all three primaries mix together, the result is a shade of brown or dull black. The mixing of all three primaries is often referred to as *mud*. If you end up with muddy colors when you want true colors, determine whether you accidentally used all three primaries in the mix. Keep in mind that these muddy colors can be beautiful and are important.

You can also create brown by mixing orange and blue or yellow and purple. Many popular colors use all three primaries—for example, a drop of red added to green creates a perfect olive green, while a drop of green added to red creates rust.

No amount of mixing can create a primary color, so be sure to stock these colors. By adding either black to shade or dust, or white to tint or pastel, in theory you can create any color of the rainbow. I say "in theory" because every brand of paint has a different way of creating pigments, and the results vary greatly. With most brands of fabric paints, greens and oranges are easy to create; however, it is difficult to create a beautiful purple. So I buy purple (and a lot of it).

If you want an exact color, test the paint on a scrap of fabric and let it dry before determining whether the color is a perfect match. I encourage you to experiment by mixing drops of paint colors on something white, such as a plastic palette. Take a little time to play and experiment to see what colors you come up with.

WHAT COLORS OF PAINT SHOULD YOU BUY?

In addition to the three primary colors of yellow, red, and blue, I suggest you buy black and white and any additional colors you use a lot of or love. If you like green, simply buy green instead of constantly using up your yellow and blue.

Fabric

Purists believe that the best fabric on which to paint is tightly woven fabric, such as pima cotton. But after years of experimenting, I've determined that I like painting on *all* types of fabrics. One of the most important attributes of paints is that they are *not* fiber sensitive. You can paint on any textile—including tightly woven or loosely woven cotton, rayon, silk, polyester, or any other textile or blend. The results will vary, but that is part of the fun!

Although it is often recommended, I have found that most fabrics do not need to be PFD (prepared for dyeing) to accept paint. The exceptions are those fabrics that contain heavy sizing, such as permanent press. Test the fabric to see if it is ready to accept paint by putting a drop of paint on the fabric. If the paint sits on top and doesn't sink in, prewash the fabric in hot water with detergent to remove any sizing.

Smoothly ironed fabric will produce the clearest images. Paint will react to wrinkles by drying in different shades as the paint penetrates the creases.

Stablized cotton, such as Cindy Walter's Stabilized Fabric (by Jacquard), works well for several painting techniques. You can easily trace or paint intricate designs on this stable fabric. As a bonus, the stabilized backing acts as a drop cloth. The backing is removed after the paint dries, exposing the back of the cotton. Stabilized cotton is made for direct painting with thick paints. It isn't useful when working with a lot of water or in such techniques as scrunching. I list it as an option, when appropriate, in several of the project supply lists.

Lutradur Flowers, by Cindy Walter, 18" × 22", 2009

It is also fun to paint on other fibers, such as Lutradur, fusible interfacing, and batting. I painted this small quilt as an experiment using Liquitex Soft Body Acrylic paint on Lutradur. I was pleasantly surprised by the results. Once dry, my Bernina easily quilted through the Lutradur to create this wall quilt.

 TIP

Have you tried Lutradur (by C&T Publishing) yet? It's a wonderful material that is being used more and more in quilting and crafts. This translucent, spun poly-ester comes in heavy, regular, and ultralight. Painted Lutradur is a great way to add texture and layers to your work. The material is porous, so be sure to put something underneath when you paint it.

Basic Supplies

This chapter lists the general supplies, in addition to paint and fabric, that you should always have handy for painting on fabric. Continue reading for more detailed information on each supply item. The projects may contain additional supplies that are unique to that project or technique.

- Apron (*optional* but useful)
- Gloves
- Drop cloth
- Brushes
- Bowls for thin paints
- Palette for thick paints
- Small container of water to dilute paints
- Water spray bottle
- Paper towels or rags
- Painting station: freezer paper or painting station board (see Make a Painting Station Board, page 14)

Apron and Gloves

Although most painting techniques are not messy, some are! The first items I suggest you grab when getting ready to paint are an apron and plastic gloves. I'm not fond of gloves, but I always wear them when handling wet paint, such as in the Scrunching technique (page 26).

Drop Cloth and Painting Station

Use a drop cloth to protect your worktable. If you are getting ready to paint, always think drop cloth first—protect the table before you start gathering your paints and other supplies. When working outside, I omit the drop cloth but still use a stack of newspapers under the paint bottles.

You can reuse the same drop cloth for months, as long as it is kept clean. I usually paint on a painting station—either pieces of freezer paper or a painting station board (see Make a Painting Station Board, page 14). In addition to keeping the drop cloth clean, the station allows me to carry the fabric to a drying area without dripping on the floor.

A painting station board is also a must for smaller, directly painted projects, such as a painted miniature quilt. It makes the project portable and allows you to turn the project to paint edges from the correct angle.

A painting station board acts as a liner to protect the drop cloth, allows you to carry wet projects to a drying area, and makes it easy to turn projects to work from different angles.

SUPPLIES

- 16" × 20" self-stick mounting board, found in the needlework or frame area of a craft store (11" × 14" for smaller projects)
- 18" × 22" clear upholstery vinyl
- Clear shipping tape

DIRECTIONS

1. Cut the vinyl to approximately 2" larger all around than the mounting board.

2. Remove the paper liner from the mounting board. Center the sticky side of the mounting board on the vinyl.

3. Turn it over so the vinyl side is up. Securely press from the center out to remove any bubbles under the vinyl. Flip it back over. Seal all four edges of the vinyl to the back of the mounting board with long pieces of shipping tape.

The painting station board will be secure enough to use over and over again. Wipe clean after each use with a damp cloth.

Brushes

Different application techniques require different brushes. Brush types are recommended in each project supply list.

If you are painting a colorwash with thin paint, use an inexpensive 1" or 2" foam brush. For a colorwash on larger pieces of fabric, use a larger brush, such as a 4" foam brush, a kitchen sponge, or a large house-painting brush.

If you are using a thick paint in a direct painting style, such as painting a miniature quilt or painting a picture, use an acrylic or oil flat brush (also called a *bright*). These brushes have short, firm bristles with which you can control heavier paints. If you only have one brush for direct painting, use a ¼"-wide flat or bright. I also use a ⅛"-wide flat in tight areas and a ½"-wide flat for larger areas. Because the undiluted opaque paint is heavy, a watercolor or soft-bristle brush is not recommended when directly painting.

Take care of your brushes. Always wash them with soap and water *immediately* after you are finished. Do not leave a brush soaking in water. Remove any excess water with a paper towel or rag. Store brushes in a jar with the bristle or foam end up. For fine artist brushes, avoid immersing the brush in the paint up to the ferrule (the metal part that holds the bristles). It is difficult to remove paint from this area, and dried paint can harm the shape of the bristles.

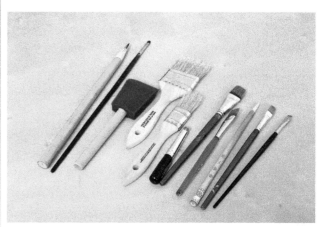

A variety of brushes

 TIP

Collect brushes of all types and sizes; you can never have too many. For some techniques, such as mono-printing (page 53), you may want to have a brayer (a hand roller used to spread paint) and a faux-finishing tool (both available in art supply and home improvement stores).

Paint Bowls, Palettes, and Water Containers

Go green—save every type of disposable container that crosses your doorstep to use as a paint bowl, palette, or water container.

For colorwashes, in which the paints are thin and often diluted with water or fabric medium, use bowls to hold the paint. Recycled cottage cheese and yogurt containers, soup cans, or to-go plastic containers make great paint bowls. Use a separate bowl for each color.

For direct painting, in which the paint is thick, use a flat palette or plate. Plastic plates, clean Styrofoam meat trays, or plastic lids make great palettes. Since you only pour tiny amounts of paint at a time, one palette per project is usually enough.

Keep a small container of fresh water handy to dilute paints.

Water Spray Bottles

A water spray bottle is needed for most colorwash techniques to dampen the fabric before painting. I always keep several bottles handy.

Pump spray bottles are also needed for the Spritzing technique (page 35). Spray bottles repurposed from every source, such as window cleaner or hair-spray bottles, will come in handy when spritzing.

Rags and Paper Towels

Paper towels or scraps of fabric are needed as cleanup rags. I also use them after washing my hands, so I don't accidently color my good bathroom towels with a dab of hidden paint. Gather the cleanup rags before even opening a bottle of paint.

 TIP

Save your cleanup rags and paper towels. Once used, spread them to dry. Iron flat. Did you create a unique masterpiece? If not, reuse as a cleanup rag.

This cleanup rag has future use in a quilt, maybe as appliqué flower petals or as part of a quilt back.

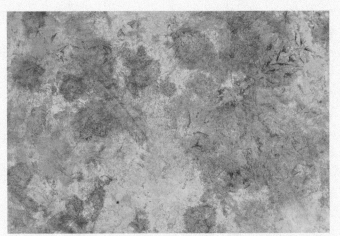

Solid white paper towels used for cleanup can be recycled. Once finished, spread out the paper towel to dry. Iron it flat and you have magically created homemade paper to use as stationary, for scrapbooking, or as wrapping paper.

Techniques and Projects

The following projects are designed to teach basic techniques. It is important for you to first read through Basic Steps for All Projects (below) and Dry or Wet? (pages 18–21). You will need this information for each project.

Basic Steps for All Projects

In addition to the individual steps in each project, follow these basic steps:

1. Put the drop cloth on your work surface before gathering the rest of the supplies.

2. Collect paints, brushes, and other supplies.

3. Fill the spray bottle and water jar with water.

4. If you are working inside, set the fabric to be painted on top of the painting station, either a piece of freezer paper or a painting board (see Make a Painting Station Board, page 14).

5. Follow the individual steps in each project.

6. After you are finished painting, wash the brushes and bowls.

7. Check to ensure all paint bottles are securely closed.

8. After the paint is dry, heat set if recommended by the manufacturer. When dry, all fabrics should be pressed before use to smooth out the wrinkles and see the striking results.

Dry or Wet?

Dry

Working dry, without diluting the paint or dampening the fabric, has a feeling that is completely different from working wet. When you want the paint to stay right where you put it, it is called *direct painting*. This look is achieved with dry fabric and thicker paint without dilution. Painting a picture and stamping are great examples of working dry or direct painting. Sometimes direct painting is as simple as spreading the paint to fill in an area.

Italian Landscape,
by Cindy Walter,
25″ × 28″, 2005

Creative souls can try using thick paints to paint an actual picture, such as a landscape. In this case, the project was painted on dry fabric without diluting paint. Use fabric medium to help blend the colors, if needed.

Wet

One of the most popular ways to use thin paints is to allow paint colors to blend together into a colorwash. Many common painting techniques start with a colorwash. This style of painting is called *wet* because water or fabric medium aids the paint's movement or blending effect.

Thin paints are meant to be used for the colorwash style of painting; however, diluting thicker paints works just as well. Diluting paints dramatically changes the results. The more dilution, the paler the resulting color. For more intense colors, use less water or medium. Dampening the fabric before painting helps the paints flow more evenly together through the damp fibers. With this technique, you'll automatically become an artist creating beautiful fabric.

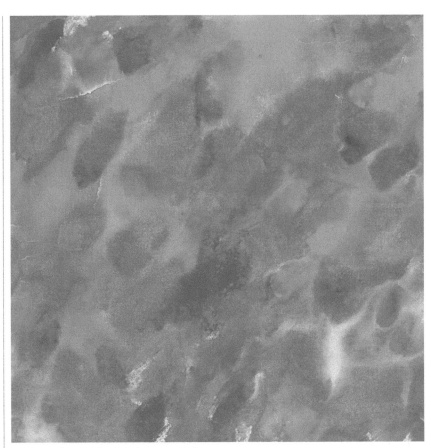

A colorwash created using the wet technique

DRY AND WET EXPERIMENTS

SUPPLIES

- 4 small pieces of white fabric
- 2 or more colors each of thick and thin paint
- 1" foam brushes—1 per paint color
- 1 bowl per paint color
- Fabric medium or matte gel medium (*optional*)

Suggested paints

Thin:

- Jacquard Dye-na-Flow
- Liquitex Acrylic Ink!
- Liquitex Soft Body Acrylic (diluted 1 part water to 2 parts paint)
- Pebeo Setasilk and Pebeo Setacolor (diluted 1 part water to 4 parts paint)

Thick:

- Liquitex Soft Body Acrylic
- Jacquard Textile or Neopaque
- Pebeo Setacolor Opaque

Directions

Refer to Basic Steps for All Projects (page 17).

PAINTING DRY

You can successfully accomplish this experiment with just one type of paint. However, if you own both transparent and opaque paints, try both on separate pieces of fabric. Start with the thick paint to keep your brush drier.

1. Pour about a tablespoon each of several colors of thick, undiluted paint into individual bowls.

2. Dip the tip of the foam brush into the first paint, and paint the color on the dry fabric.

3. Paint the remaining colors, filling in the white areas. Notice how difficult it is to blend colors. You can also do this test by adding a fabric medium to each color for a variation.

Dry fabric painted with undiluted Liquitex Soft Body Acrylic paints—the thick paint stays where it is brushed on dry fabric.

4. Repeat Steps 1–3 of the experiment with new fabric, bowls, and brushes to test the thin paints.

Dry fabric painted with undiluted Jacquard Dye-na-Flow paint—the thin paints blend together, but only slightly.

PAINTING WET

1. Use the same paint bowls and corresponding brushes as in the dry experiment. Replenish the thick paint so there is about a tablespoon of thick paint in each bowl.

2. Dilute the thick paint with 1 part water to 1 part paint; the amount varies by brand, so experiment.

3. Spray a new piece of fabric with water so it is quite damp.

4. Repeat the first experiment by painting the colors around the fabric. Notice how easily the colors blend.

5. A fabric medium is most helpful in this situation. I like to dilute thicker paints with fabric medium in addition to water. The medium allows you to spread the thicker paint without resistance. Test first with water; then use a medium to see the variation. Feel free to experiment with the amount of fabric medium you use; it all depends on the desired look. As a starting point for this experiment, try using 2 parts paint to 1 part Liquitex Fabric Medium.

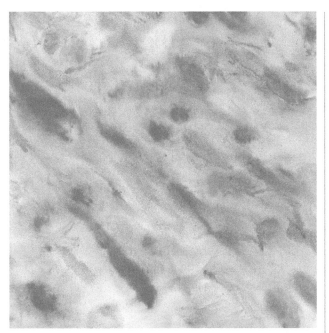

Fabric dampened with water and Liquitex Soft Body Acrylic paints diluted with water and fabric medium—see how the thick paints now blend?

6. Repeat the experiment to test the thinner paint. Dilute the thin paint with 1 part water to 2 parts paint. Be sure to dampen all the fabrics before painting.

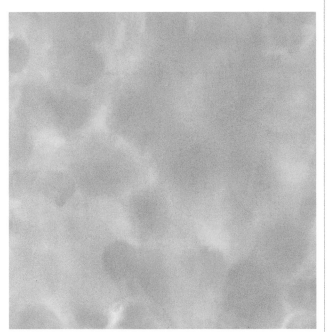

Fabric dampened with water and painted with diluted Jacquard Dye-na-Flow—the thin paints flow together, resulting in a beautiful colorwash.

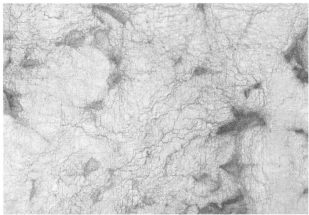

The spider veins on this fabric were created by using thin, transparent paint with extra water, which broke down the paint's binder, or base. Experiment by using more water than paint. Because the paint is still permanent and washable, these lines become a bonus for us fiber artists, adding texture and character to the fabric.

While experimenting with dry or wet painting techniques, try different brushstrokes.

Did you like working dry or wet? I primarily like working with wet fabric because I love to watch the paint magically disperse through the wet fibers. Of course, there are times when I don't want the paint to disperse; in that case, dry is the best. Did you notice the variation in the intensity of the colors after the paint dried? The more water or medium added to the paint, the lighter the resulting color.

Colorwash

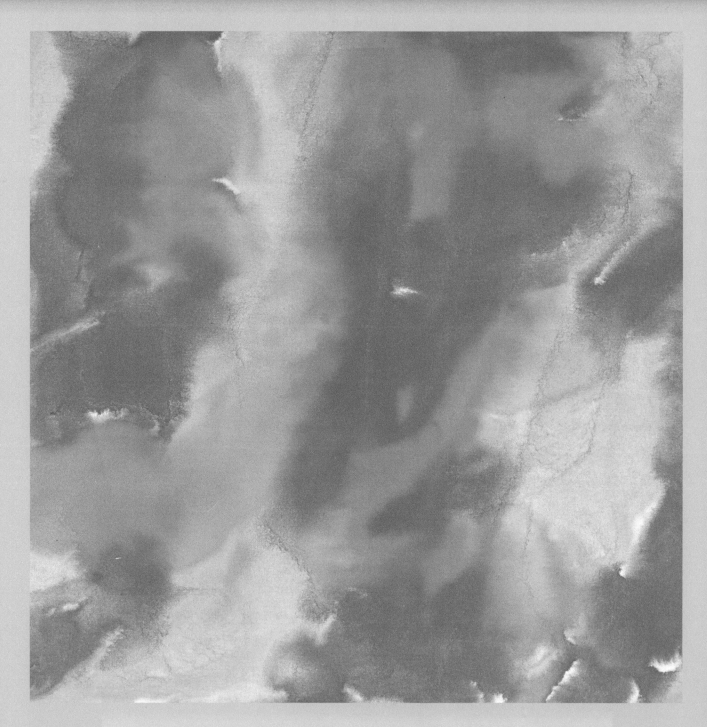

Colorwash is a common technique using fabric paints. Its beauty can rival (or exceed) the best commercial fabrics. Although colorwashing makes a great background fabric for quilt projects, don't think of it as simply a background. Instead, think of it as creating fabric for every need. For instance, you can paint the perfect fabric for the petals of an appliquéd flower or a brilliant blue for the center of your pieced star. You can even paint yardage for your custom-designed home decor projects or garments.

SUPPLIES

- White fabric (any size)

- 2 or more colors thin paint (or diluted thick paint)

- 1 foam brush per paint color

- 1 bowl per paint color

- Fabric medium (*optional*)

Suggested paints

- Jacquard Dye-na-Flow

- Liquitex Acrylic Ink!

- Liquitex Soft Body Acrylic (diluted 1 part water to 2 parts paint)

- Pebeo Setasilk

- Pebeo Setacolor (diluted 1 part water to 4 parts paint)

Directions

Refer to Basic Steps for All Projects (page 17).

notes

- *For the best wash effect, use a water spray bottle to dampen fabric before painting. The wet fibers help the paint flow.*

- *You can mix metallic paints with the recommended paints to create highlights. Use them sparingly in this technique.*

- *For a good colorwash effect, work quickly without taking a break between colors.*

✺ TIP

Remember, results vary depending on the brand of paint and the amount of water used. Don't be afraid; this is play. There is no right or wrong, just different results.

✺ TIP

I waited five minutes between painting three sets of brushstrokes. Notice the dark echo lines where the paint dried. For a smooth, blended effect, keep fabric damp and do not take breaks between colors.

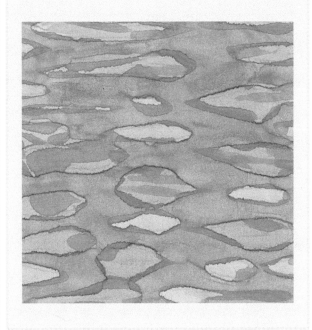

1. Pour approximately a tablespoon of each color into separate bowls. Dilute with water, if necessary, so the paint has a milky consistency.

2. Completely dampen the fabric with a spray of water.

3. Dip the foam brush into the first color. Randomly dab the brush on the fabric to spread the paint. The brushstrokes or dabs of paint can be done in any pattern.

Begin applying the paint.

4. Dip a clean foam brush into the next color. Spread the paint around the fabric, while filling in some of the white areas. Slightly overlap the first color.

Apply the second color of paint.

5. Spray the fabric with more water if needed to help the paint blend.

6. Spread the final color around the fabric, filling in the rest of the white areas. Slightly overlap the first colors. Stop painting when you are satisfied with the results. Do not overwork the process.

Apply the final color of paint.

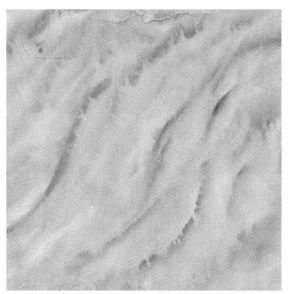

Paint a wash with just one color or stay within a color family.

Try a wash with many colors.

A multicolored colorwash is the perfect way to dress up a white canvas bag.

UGLY DUCKLINGS TO SWANS

Remember that one advantage of paint is that you can paint on any fabric—even fabric already commercially printed. In one of my workshops, we collect "ugly duckling" fabrics and challenge each other to turn them into swans. Not that I'd call any fabrics ugly—they just need a little dressing up.

Paint can also enhance the natural beauty of fabrics that are not ugly ducklings. Black-and-white and white-on-white fabrics are especially fun to paint. Every quilt shop has at least one of these on sale, making them as cheap as white cotton.

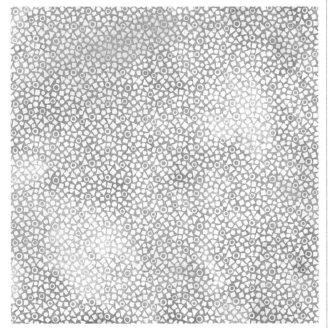

Painting over commercial white-on-white prints provides interesting results.

Adding paint to a black-and-white print fabric yields a totally new look.

Scrunching

When experimenting, if all else fails, scrunch it! This is truly the easiest painting technique. Simply paint a colorwash (page 22), scrunch it, and leave it to dry. It is a delight to open the scrunched fabric to find unexpected, beautiful character markings.

SUPPLIES

- Fabric (any size)

- 2 or more colors thin paint (or diluted thick paint)

- 1 foam brush per paint color

- 1 bowl per paint color

Suggested paints

- Jacquard Dye-na-Flow

- Liquitex Acrylic Ink!

- Liquitex Soft Body Acrylic (diluted 1 part water to 2 parts paint)

- Pebeo Setasilk

- Pebeo Setacolor (diluted 1 part water to 4 parts paint)

Directions

Refer to Basic Steps for All Projects (page 17).

notes

Where the paint takes longer to dry (in the valleys), the pigment is lighter. Where the paint dries quickly (in the peak), the pigment is bolder.

Rescrunching the fabric several times while it is drying will add more character marks to the fabric.

To create a great colorwash, use a water spray bottle to dampen fabric. The wet fibers help the paint blend.

Use metallic paints sparingly in this technique, because they don't flow well.

1. Use as many colors as you choose to paint a colorwash (page 22). Be liberal with the water.

Start with a pink and yellow colorwash, and then add a touch of olive.

2. Immediately scrunch the fabric. Then leave it to dry on a drop cloth or piece of freezer paper set out of the way. Drying can take several hours or even overnight.

Scrunched fabric

3. Rescrunch the fabric every hour or so to add extra character to the fabric.

4. After the fabric is completely dry, open it up to reveal the beautiful patterns.

Dried scrunched fabric from previous page

Purple and yellow wash is nice, but less than stunning.

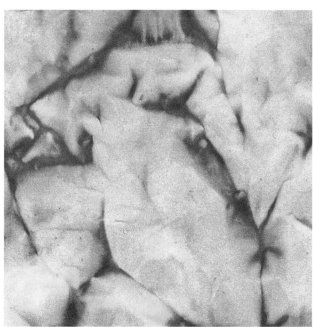

Purple and yellow wash scrunched yields striking results.

This white cotton shirt was painted with a bright scrunch of pinks and yellow.

Salting

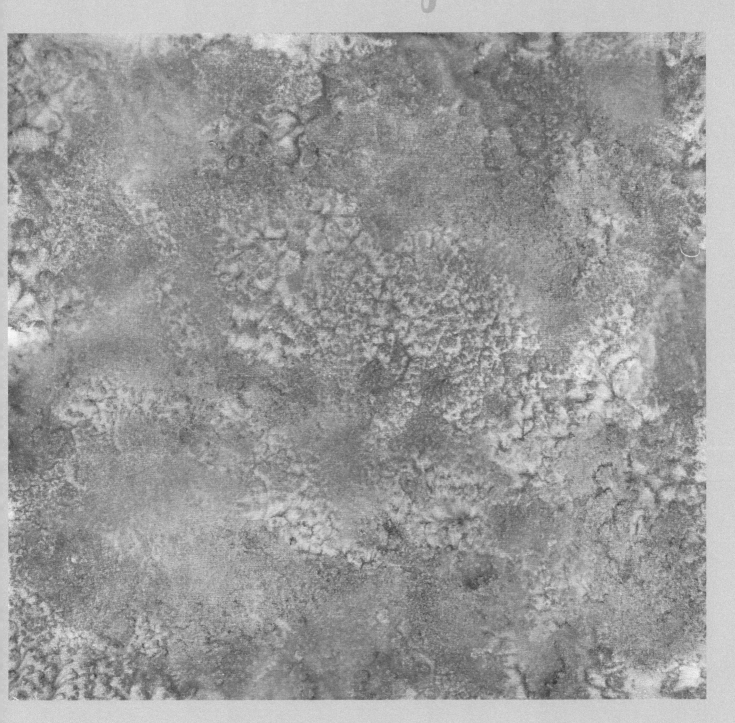

With its beautiful bursts of color, this fabric can be used in any patchwork, home decor project, or garment. It is a great project for the outdoors or with children. For this technique, it is important to use transparent paints (page 8).

- Fabric—looser weave, such as bleached muslin (any size)
- Salt (rock or sea)
- Thin transparent paints
- 1 foam brush per paint color
- 1 bowl per paint color

Suggested paints

- Jacquard Dye-na-Flow (diluted 1 part water to 2 parts paint)
- Liquitex Acrylic Ink! (diluted 1 part water to 2 parts paint)
- Liquitex Soft Body Acrylic transparent colors (diluted 3 parts water to 4 parts paint)
- Pebeo Setasilk
- Pebeo Setacolor Transparent (diluted 1 part water to 2 parts paint)

Directions

Refer to Basic Steps for All Projects (page 17).

notes

Use larger rock or sea salt for great results. Medium grains, such as salt for grinders and kosher salt, also work. Table salt is the least preferred, as it forms only a light haze on the fabric.

Looser-weave fabrics, such as bleached muslin, work better than tighter weaves, such as cotton sateen, because the salt has to pull the water through the fabric fibers. Silk salts beautifully.

For the best salt effects, dilute the paints with a little more water than normal. The fabric must be damp before painting. The wet fibers help the salt draw up the paint.

Use metallic paints sparingly. Although these thicker paints can be made into a thin consistency by diluting them, they have heavy molecules and thus do not respond well to salt.

1. Spray the fabric with water to dampen it. Paint a colorwash (page 22). Be liberal with the water.

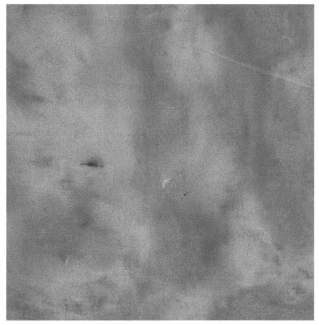

Paint a colorwash.

2. Immediately sprinkle salt on the fabric. If the salt doesn't become translucent with the water from the paint, spray the salt with a small amount of water. Let it dry.

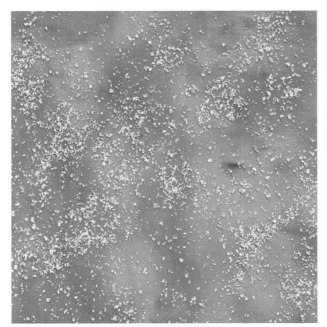

Place salt on colorwashed fabric.

3. After the paint is completely dry, brush off the salt. You can save the salt in a plastic bag and reuse it for your next project. If the salt is difficult to remove from the fabric, let the fabric dry for several weeks to cure the paint, then rinse away the salt.

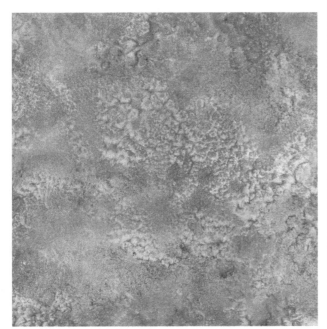

It is magic! The salt pulls the water, leaving stunning marks in the paint.

Teal silk scarf with large rock salt marks, 9″ × 53″

Front: Salt cannot easily pull the paint on fabric that is painted with metallic and opaque paints.

Back: Notice that it did pull some of the paint, just not the heavier, thicker metallic and opaque paint on the top of the fabric.

Heliography (Sun Printing)

Heliographed Garden, by Cindy Walter, 60″ × 60″, 2009

Heliography, also known as sun printing, is an ancient technique. In fact, it is a precursor to photography. This perfect project for children is done outdoors on a sunny, windless day. For this technique, it is important to use transparent paints (page 8).

SUPPLIES

- White fabric

- Items for imaging, such as leaves, flowers, rice, and so forth

- Several colors of thin transparent paint

- 1 foam brush per paint color

- 1 bowl per paint color

Suggested paints

- Jacquard Dye-na-Flow (diluted 1 part water to 2 parts paint)

- Liquitex Acrylic Ink! (diluted 1 part water to 2 parts paint)

- Liquitex Soft Body Acrylic transparent colors (diluted 3 parts water to 4 parts paint)

- Pebeo Setasilk

- Pebeo Setacolor Transparent (diluted 1 part water to 2 parts paint)

Directions

Refer to Basic Steps for All Projects (page 17).

notes

Collect the image items ahead of time. Anything that lies flat on wet paint will heliograph. Think about items from nature, your food pantry, or even your toolbox. You must collect these items before starting to paint.

Use metallic paints sparingly. Although these thicker paints can be diluted to a thin consistency, they don't respond well to heliography.

I paint right on the grass, without a drop cloth. I set my paint bottles and bowls on a stack of newspapers.

 TIP

The only rule for image items is that they must lie flat on the fabric. A slightly curled dried leaf will not work, because the air will flow underneath and prematurely dry the paint.

I once held a workshop with children in which we only used items from the food pantry: Cheerios, macaroni, rice, and beans. Very fun! You can even use letters or motifs cut from cardboard.

1. Spray the fabric with water to dampen it. Paint a colorwash (page 22).

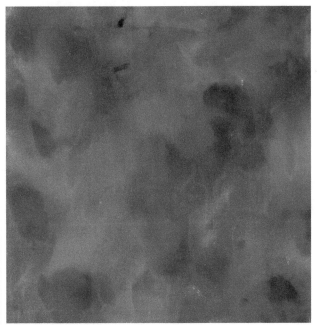

Start with a colorwash.

2. Immediately place the image items on the wet fabric. (For this example, I wanted to imprint my fabric with circles. I almost decided to use coins, but then I found a box of metal washers in my husband's toolbox. He'll never miss them—anything for the success of art!)

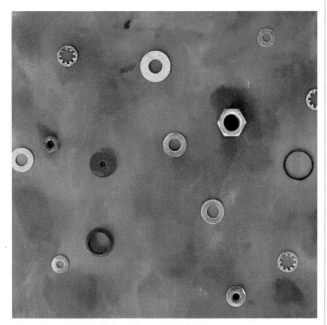

Place image items on the colorwashed fabric.

3. Leave the fabric to dry in the bright sun. Don't peek!

4. When the fabric is dry, remove the items to reveal the heliographic images.

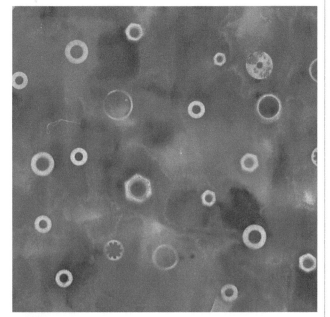

Finished fabric

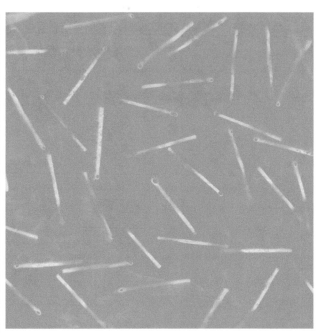

Fabric heliographed with wooden matchsticks

I was pleasantly surprised to find these flowers blanketing the backyard of a quilt shop where I held a workshop in Brisbane, Australia. Can any of my Aussie friends name these white flowers?

Spritzing

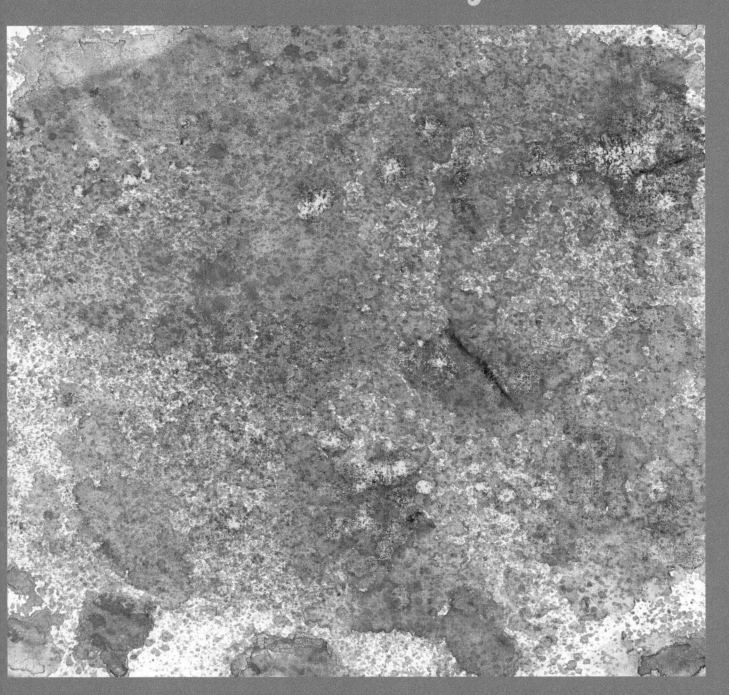

This is a fast painting technique for outside on a windless day. It is also a great method to paint three-dimensional items. Save different types of spray bottles—from old hair-spray pumps to spray cleaner bottles.

- Any size, type, or color fabric

- Any type, any color paint

- Several plastic spray bottles—1 for each paint color is helpful.

- Small funnel (*optional*)

- Clothesline with clothespins (*optional* but helpful)

Directions

Refer to Basic Steps for All Projects (page 17).

notes

This technique is for outdoors on a windless day. The free-spirited nature of this technique is perfect for kids.

All varieties of paints work. You may have to thin the thicker varieties if they won't spray through the nozzle.

If possible, hang the fabric from a clothesline to get an even spray. You can also drape the fabric on a bush, or simply place it on the grass.

Collect and repurpose used spray bottles, from hairspray to window cleaner bottles. Rinse them out well after spritzing to prevent the tube from clogging.

Some spray bottles spray fine mists, while others spray large splatters. Test the bottles with water. Note on the bottle's side with a permanent pen what type of pattern it creates.

Be sure the spray tube reaches the inside bottom of the bottle; otherwise you'll waste ounces of paint. Although you can't pour unused paint back in the paint bottle, you can rinse the spray bottle with a little water and use the diluted paint for a colorwash (page 22).

1. Pour a few tablespoons of paint in a spray bottle. Make sure the paint level rises above the bottom of the spray tube.

2. Test the spray on a piece of scrap fabric or paper towel. Thin the paint with water, if necessary.

3. Pin the pieces of fabrics on a clothesline or drape them over a bush.

4. Spritz the first color on the fabric until you achieve the desired coverage.

5. Add the next colors. Stop when you are happy with the results. Let the fabric dry.

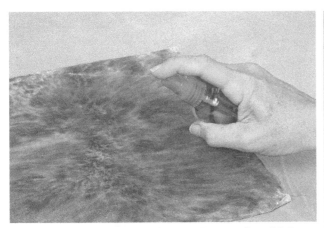

This blending effect was achieved by spritzing onto damp fabric.

Spritzing was a fast way to paint this silk tie, especially since I didn't want to take the risk of the silk shrinking by getting the project completely wet.

Spritzing is the best way to paint three-dimensional objects, such as this stuffed cat.

Almost Shibori

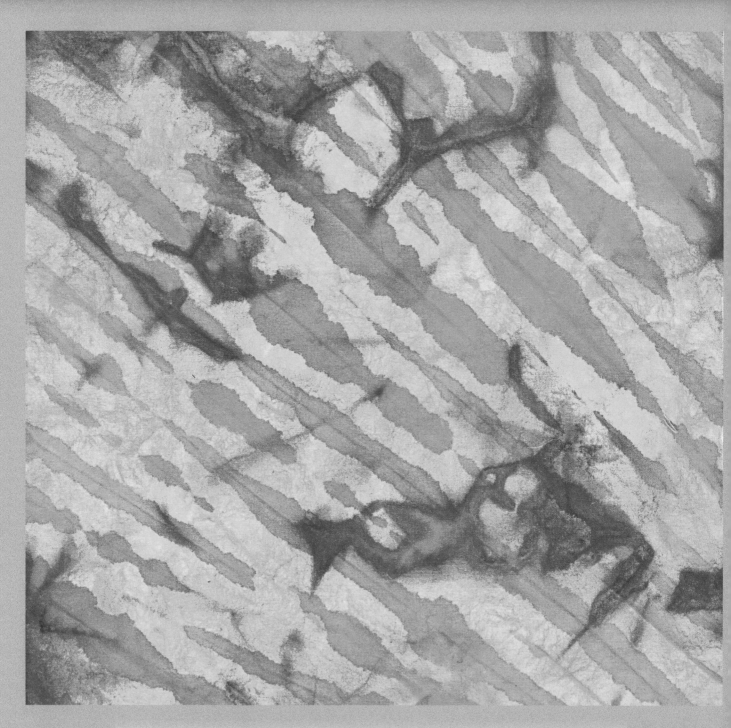

Shibori originated in China, though it is rarely practiced there today. When you say *shibori*, you think Japan. Japan cultivated the technique in which fabric is wrapped, twisted, and bound to create striking patterns on cloth. Shibori is commonly used with dye, though it also works in a subtle manner with paint. There are many ways to wrap the fabric—after all, that is the secret of shibori. The technique shown in this project is the easiest for a beginner.

- Any size, type, or color of fabric, you want to change

- Strong rubber band

- Thin paints

- 1 foam brush per paint color

- 1 bowl per paint color

Suggested paints

- Jacquard's Dye-na-Flow (diluted 1 part water to 2 parts paint)

- Liquitex Acrylic Ink! (diluted 1 part water to 4 parts paint)

- Liquitex Soft Body Acrylic (diluted 3 parts water to 4 parts paint)

- Pebeo Setasilk (diluted 1 part water to 4 parts paint)

- Pebeo Setacolor (diluted 1 part water to 2 parts paint)

Directions

Refer to Basic Steps for All Projects (page 17).

notes

□ *There are many wrapping methods, such as* arashi *(wrapping on a pole) and* mandala *(creating a pattern from the center out). Books on shibori are suggested in Resources (page 78).*

□ *This is a perfect technique for adding additional character to any piece of fabric you've already painted.*

□ *Opaque paints or metallic paints can be used for certain effects, but they are not ideal.*

1. Start with either white or colored fabric. I started with a piece of pink and green fabric that had been painted with a colorwash (page 22) and then scrunched (page 26).

Start with plain or prepainted fabric.

2. Fold the fabric on the diagonal, accordion style, with the folds about an inch thick.

Fold the fabric accordion style.

3. Fold the resulting piece accordion style again.

Fold the fabric accordion style again.

4. Secure the folded fabric with a rubber band.

Secure with a rubber band.

5. Pour thin paint into a bowl. Use a foam brush to paint the folded edges of the fabric roll.

Paint the fabric edges.

6. Let the fabric roll dry completely. Then open it to reveal the shibori pattern (see photo, page 38).

7. After the fabric is dry, you can add more color by folding it again on the diagonal from the other angle.

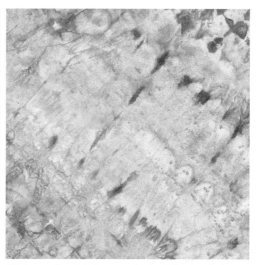

Silk is a perfect fabric to use in the shibori technique.

Shibori silk scarf, by Cindy Walter, 9½" × 43", 2010

Painted Miniature
Dutchman's Puzzle

Miniature Dutchman's Puzzle, by Cindy Walter, 7″ × 8″, 2010

Painting a miniature quilt is as easy as painting by numbers. The only secret is to evenly spread the paint on the fabric. This project is directly painted with thick, opaque paint (page 9) without water. You need a short, strong brush, such as a ¼″-wide flat. This fast, fun project will impress your friends, who will actually want to touch your quilt, refusing to believe it is painted and not pieced.

- Painting station board (*optional but* very helpful, page 14)

- 9″ × 8″ white cotton, such as Cindy Walter's Stabilized Cotton (Resources, page 78); or 8½″ × 11″ pretreated cotton sheets for use in inkjet printers and an inkjet printer

- 3 colors thick opaque paint

- ¼″-wide flat acrylic brush

- ⅛″-wide flat brush (*optional* but helpful)

- Palette or plate

Suggested paints

- Liquitex Soft Body Acrylic opaque

- Jacquard Textile and Lumiere

- Pebeo Setacolor or Pebeo Setacolor Opaque

Directions

Refer to Basic Steps for All Projects (page 17).

notes

  Use thick, opaque, undiluted paint. Because you must control where the paint flows, do not use thin paint or liquid ink.

  Also try the permanent ink pens for fabric on this project. Jacquard's Tee Juices fine tip or the bullet end of Tsukineko's Fabrico pens are excellent tools to color in tiny areas such as the patchwork pieces in this quilt. These pens are easy to use and can interchange with paints. They must be heat set with a hot dry iron.

  Work on dry fabric with a dry brush. It is important that you use a firm flat brush rather than a soft bristle watercolor brush.

PREPARATION

Use one of the options below to photocopy or trace the miniature quilt pattern (page 76) to the fabric.

Photocopying: This is the fastest way to transfer the pattern. Use an all-in-one inkjet printer to copy the pattern onto a piece of cotton fabric pretreated for use in inkjet printers. Do not use untreated cotton in the printer, as the ink would run when washed. Keep the paper backing on the inkjet cotton until you are finished painting, as it will act as a stabilizer.

Tracing: Tape the pattern to a window or backlit source, such as a lightbox. Tape a piece of stabilized cotton on top of the pattern and trace with a pencil. Keep the paper backing on the stabilized cotton until you are finished painting, as it will act as a stabilizer.

PAINTING

1. Select a paint color for each section of patchwork.

2. Pour ½ teaspoon of the first color onto your plate or palette. Dip the tip of your flat brush into the paint and spread the paint as thinly as possible in the corresponding patchwork areas. Start at the center of the quilt to avoid dragging your hand across wet paint as you rotate the project. Paint all the areas of the first color.

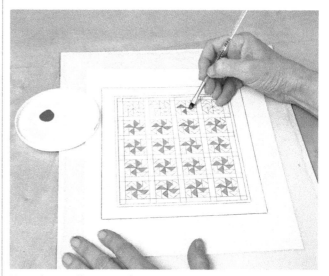

Use only a small amount of paint on the brush tip.

3. To achieve sharp edges, lay the brush at a 45° angle, parallel to the pencil line, and spread the paint with a side-to-side motion along the edge until the edge line of the pattern piece is straight. Rotate the project so your hand is at the correct angle to reach each edge. When painting the center of any area, *pull* the paint with the brush flat rather than using the side-to-side motion. Reserve the side-to-side motion for the edges—this motion will eventually damage the brush and should thus be used only when necessary.

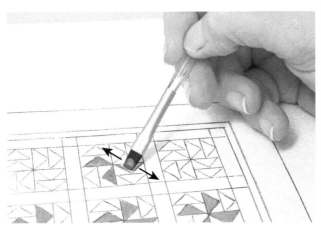

A back-and-forth motion at a 45° angle creates a straight line.

4. Let the first color of paint dry for a few minutes before starting the next color. Wash and dry the brush and palette between colors. Remember to use tiny amounts of paint on the tip of your brush and to spread the paint as thinly as possible.

Paint the second color.

A 10″ × 14″ painting station board is especially handy in this project, as you will want to rotate the entire project to get the correct angle when painting the inside of each line.

5. Paint the last color, ending with the outer border. The border is the one area in which you can be nice to your brush. Because the tiny patchwork areas of this project use mostly side-to-side brushstrokes, be sure to pull the brush on the large areas of the border.

Pulling the brush in this manner is easier on the bristles.

6. If you used inkjet fabric or stabilized cotton, remove the paper backing once the paint is dry.

7. You are ready to turn your project into a quilt. Layer, baste, and quilt as desired. Bind the edges.

> ❋ **TIP**
>
> *If a tiny splash of paint hits an area where it shouldn't, let the paint dry and then overpaint with the correct color. You can also use white paint to cover an area before repainting with the correct color. Although this is not a perfect fix, it will usually do the trick for small errors. If you make a **large mistake**, you'll need to change the design and paint that portion of the quilt with the "mistaken" color. Even a "mistake" can become part of a beautiful design.*

Star Burst Compass, by Cindy Walter, 10" × 10", 2008

Another painted quilt—the pattern is available from JWD Publishing (see Resources, page 78).

Painting is finished.

Painted Hawaiian Quilt

Akala—Hawaiian Raspberry, by Cindy Walter, 14" × 14", 2010

Living in Hawaii makes it easy to find inspirations to design Hawaiian quilt patterns. I designed this pattern without the traditional lei border. As much as I enjoy the traditional Hawaiian needle-turn method, I couldn't resist painting this quilt in an "akala" (the Hawaiian word for raspberry) color.

This project is rewarding and fast. It is directly painted, so there is no guesswork. Simply spread the paint as evenly as possible within the lines. Your friends will be shocked by the beauty of the finished project, and they will not believe the design is painted and not appliquéd. Highlight the painting with machine quilting, using the traditional echo pattern, to get a quilt with a true Hawaiian feeling.

SUPPLIES

- Painting station board (*optional but very helpful, page 14*)

- 14″ × 14″ white cotton or 14″ × 14″ stabilized cotton

- 1 color opaque acrylic thick fabric paint

- ¼″-wide flat acrylic brush (firm; *not* soft like a watercolor brush)

- 3 pieces 8½″ × 11″ white plain paper

- Pencil

- Scissors

- Tape

- Palette or plate

Suggested paints

- Liquitex Soft Body Acrylic opaque

- Jacquard Textile and Lumiere

- Pebeo Setacolor Opaque

Directions

Refer to Basic Steps for All Projects (page 17).

notes

■ *Hawaiian quilt tops are made by folding fabric into eighths, like a pie wedge. The pattern is then pinned on top of the fabric wedge, and the entire quilt top is cut out at once—snowflake style. The following pattern is the typical eighths pie wedge design. However, you are not cutting out the appliqué fabric; instead, you will trace the pattern onto fabric. Because it is more accurate to use a full-size template, you must first trace the pattern (page 77) onto folded paper and then cut it out to make your template.*

■ *Use thick, undiluted paint; you must control where the paint flows when painting this miniature quilt.*

■ *Work on dry fabric with a dry brush. It is important that you use a firm flat brush rather than a soft bristle brush, which is meant for watercolor.*

PREPARATION

1. Photocopy or trace the pattern (page 77).

2. To make a full-size pattern, tape two 8½″ × 11″ pieces of white paper together to create one large piece of paper that measures 17″ × 11″. Fold the paper in half to create a rectangle (8½″ × 11″) and then fold it a second time (8½″ × 5½″). Fold this piece on the diagonal at the fold to create an eighth pie wedge angle.

3. Place the pattern on top of the folded paper, lining up the fold lines and the center tip. A lightbox or sunny window may help you line up the fold lines on the pattern with the folded paper edges. Tape or use spray adhesive to hold the pattern securely to the folded paper.

Tape or glue the pattern to the folded fabric.

4. Cut out the pattern along the "cut only" lines.

Cut out the pattern.

5. Unfold to view the completed paper template. Transfer the template to the fabric by taping it to a window or lightbox. Tape the cotton on top of the template and trace it with a pencil.

Trace the pattern onto cloth.

PAINTING

1. Pour ½ teaspoon of paint onto your plate or palette. Dip the tip of your brush into the paint and spread the paint as thinly as possible in the appliqué area.

Painting the appliqué

2. To get sharp edges, hold the brush at a 45° angle, parallel to the pencil line, and spread the paint in a side-to-side motion, painting a smooth edge line of the appliqué. Rotate the project to reach the inside of each edge. A large painting station board (page 14) is especially handy in this project, because it allows you to continually rotate the project so you can paint the inside of each edge from the correct angle.

Be sure to hold the brush at a 45° angle, parallel to the pencil line, when painting the edges.

3. When painting the center of any design area, *pull* the paint with the brush flat, rather than using the side-to-side motion. Reserve the side-to-side motion for the edges, as this motion will eventually damage the bristles and thus should be used only when necessary.

The finished painting

4. If you use stabilized cotton, remove the paper backing once the paint is dry.

5. You are ready to turn your project into a quilt. Layer and baste. The traditional Hawaiian quilting line is a finger's-width echo around the appliqué design. Continue to quilt an echo all the way to the quilt's edge. Finish the edge.

 TIP

The traditional Hawaiian quilting technique is to echo the design without drawing quilting lines. Experiment with your machine. I have found that with my Bernina, using a walking foot with the feed dogs up but with a lower pressure on the presser foot (see your sewing machine manual) allows me to quilt curves, while keeping the echo lines a consistent distance from one another. If you can't release the presser foot pressure, then you will have to use a darning foot with the feed dogs down and then free-motion quilt to maneuver the curves.

Hawaiian Pineapple Quilt, by Cindy Walter, 25" × 25", 2006

I found this Pineapple pattern in *Menehune Quilts,* by Elizabeth Root, a famous Hawaiian quilt pattern designer. I immediately realized that all the quilt patterns in her book are perfect for the direct-painting technique, because they are compact and have a lot of details. See more examples at www.quiltshawaii.com.

Painted
Flowers with Resist

Painted Flowers, by Cindy Walter, 24" × 28", 2010

This project, which combines the two basic painting techniques of colorwash (page 22) and direct painting (page 45), is a great learning tool. The background is painted with a colorwash after first protecting the flower design with a resist. Then the flowers are painted.

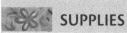

- 18″ × 22″ white cotton or stabilized cotton

- Thin paints—blue and purple

- Thick opaque paints—cherry, pink, white, yellow, and 2 greens

- Clear gutta resist (or beeswax) with applicator (*If the gutta resist does not come with a built-in applicator, use a syringe.*)

- 1 foam brush for each thin paint color

- 1 bowl for each thin color

- ¼″-wide flat acrylic brush

- Palette or plate for opaque paints

Suggested paints

Thin:

- Jacquard's Dye-na-Flow (diluted 1 part water to 4 parts paint)

- Liquitex Acrylic Ink! (diluted 1 part water to 4 parts paint)

- Liquitex Soft Body Acrylic (diluted 1 part water to 2 parts paint)

- Pebeo Setasilk

- Pebeo Setacolor (diluted 1 part water to 4 parts paint)

Thick:

- Liquitex Soft Body Acrylic opaque

- Jacquard Textile and Lumiere

- Pebeo Setacolor Opaque

Directions

Refer to Basic Steps for All Projects (page 17).

notes

■ *Read the directions completely before starting. The resist prevents the background paint from entering the flower areas. The timing is important, as you must allow the resist to dry before painting the colorwash.*

■ *There are several resists on the market, so use whatever is available. I use Jacquard Gutta Resist (Resources, page 78) and a syringe. Beeswax also works well. Some brands of gutta come in a convenient squeeze tube.*

PREPARATION

1. Enlarge the flower pattern (page 77) 400% on a copy machine and trace it onto the fabric, or simply freehand draw the flowers with a pencil directly on the fabric.

2. Using an applicator, draw a thick line of gutta or beeswax resist on top of the pencil lines. Be sure to make each line a closed loop so the motifs stay free of background paint.

3. Allow the gutta or beeswax to dry completely before painting. This will take at least an hour.

Apply the resist and let it dry.

PAINTING

1. Pour about a tablespoon of thin blue paint into a bowl. Pour an equal amount of thin purple paint in a separate bowl. Check to make sure the bottle lids are securely closed. Remember to dilute paint with water (see Supplies, page 50).

2. Lightly spray the background fabric with water, avoiding the flower areas.

3. Paint a colorwash (page 22). You must work fast when painting this colorwash. Think of painting the two colors as one step to achieve a nice blend of color.

Paint the background colorwash.

4. Allow the colorwash background to completely dry. You are now finished with the thin paints. Wash the bowls and brushes.

5. To paint the flowers, pour a teaspoon each of cherry, red, white, and yellow on a palette or plate. Start with the cherry and red to paint the outside area of the flower petal. To get sharp edges, lay the brush at a 45° angle, parallel to the pencil line, and spread the paint in a side-to-side motion. Rotate the project to reach all the inside edges.

Hold the brush at a 45° angle, parallel to the pencil line.

6. Blend white into the center areas. A tiny dab of water or fabric medium on the tip of your brush will help the colors blend. When painting the center of any area, *pull* the paint with the brush flat, rather than using the side-to-side motion described in Step 5.

Blend the white into the cherry and red.

7. After the flowers are finished, paint tiny dashes of yellow in the petal near the flower center.

Add dashes of yellow.

8. Pour about a teaspoon of each color of green paint on the palette. Paint the leaves. Shade one side of the leaves with the darkest green.

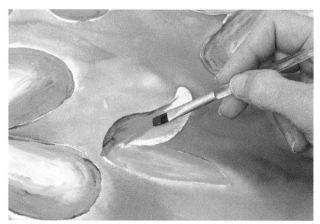

Paint the leaves.

9. While the green is still wet, use red or your darkest color to highlight the leaves with veins. The red will blend with the green to create a rusty shade of brown.

Add veins to the leaves.

10. If you used stabilized cotton, remove the paper backing once the paint is dry.

11. Add borders and embellish with stencils (page 59), if desired.

12. Layer, baste, quilt, and finish the edges.

TIP

Have fun when finishing your painted quilts. This is a perfect project on which to stencil, stamp or even machine embroider. You can use commercially printed fabric for the borders, but I used more paint techniques to add depth and interest. Quilting through painted fabric is the same as quilting regular patchwork. I use a machine quilting needle size 10 and thread designed for machine quilting.

I embellished the background with stenciled dragonflies. The inner border in my project is a piece of painted green fabric. The outer blue border is heliographed with leaves to match the flower theme. Playful quilting lines finish the project.

Monoprinting

Monoprinting is the process of making a single print using a printing plate. The paint is applied to the plate and then pressed to the fabric.

SUPPLIES

- Upholstery vinyl for printing plate

- Any size or type of fabric, white or previously painted

- 1 or more colors thick opaque or metallic paint

- Foam brush, bristle brush, brayer, or scrunched paper towel to apply paint

- Additional items, such as faux-finishing tools, to make marks on the paint

- Palette or plate

Suggested paints

- Liquitex Soft Body Acrylic

- Jacquard Textile or Lumiere

- Pebeo Setacolor Opaque

Directions

Refer to Basic Steps for All Projects (page 17).

notes

■ *Clear, flexible vinyl is easy to use for monoprinting, but you can also use glass, Plexiglas, plastic tablecloth, or any other smooth surface that will lie flat and is waterproof.*

■ *Some artists find it helpful to work on a padded surface, such as a piece of batting. I prefer working with the fabric directly on the table.*

■ *A paint roller, also called a brayer, is a great tool to apply a smoother layer of paint or to paint over uneven surfaces, such as Bubble Wrap.*

■ *Mix paint with medium to extend your working time.*

1. Pour a small amount of the desired paint colors on the palette or plate.

2. Apply paint to the vinyl. You can paint a design or just create textures.

Apply paint to the vinyl.

3. Place the printing plate (vinyl) paint side down onto dry fabric. Press evenly.

4. Carefully lift to reveal the design.

Carefully lift the vinyl. I applied my flowers to a piece of prepainted blue fabric that I found on my "reject" pile.

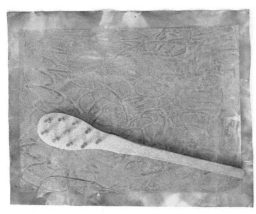

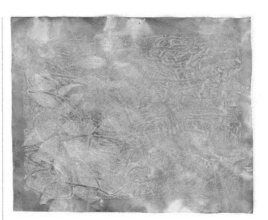

Another style of monoprinting is to apply a thin, even layer of paint to the printing plate using a brush or brayer. Then draw a pattern in the smooth layer of paint using a tool such as a notched spackle spreader or a spaghetti ladle.

Monoprinted fabric

Tulips, by Cindy Walter, 7" × 9", 2010

A monoprint of tulips makes a perfect design for a small, festive quilt.

Stamping

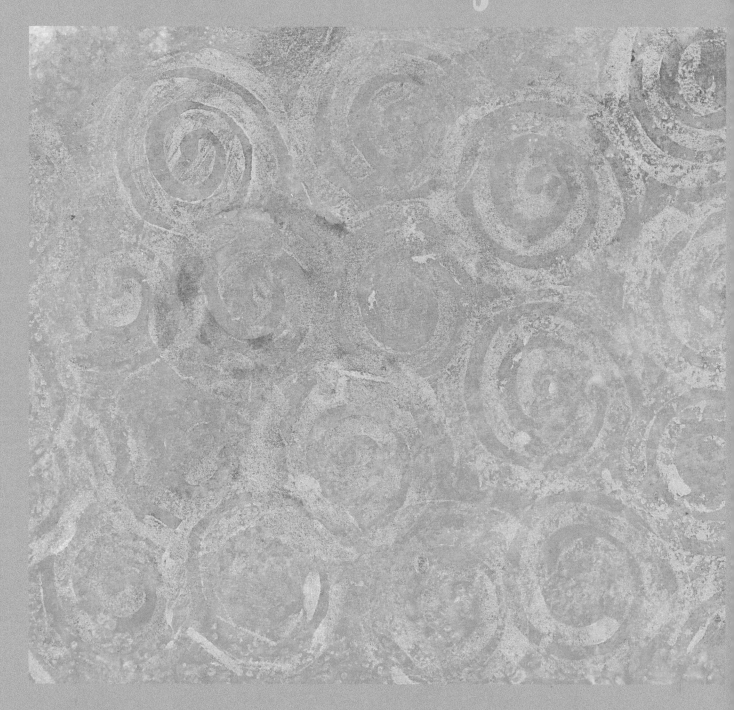

Stamping is a fast way to add embellishment to any type of project, from a pillow to a bed quilt. Rubber stamps of every design are available. You can also easily make your own.

SUPPLIES

- Any size or type of fabric, white or already colored

- Opaque or metallic paint, 1 or more colors

- Rubber stamps

- ½"-wide stencil brush or small foam brush

Suggested paints

- Liquitex Soft Body Acrylic

- Jacquard Textile or Lumiere

- Pebeo Setacolor or Setacolor Opaque

Directions

Refer to Basic Steps for All Projects (page 17).

notes

- *Work on dry fabric with a dry brush.*

- *Some artists find it helpful to work on a padded surface, such as a piece of batting. I get crisper results without a padded surface.*

1. Use a brush to dab paint onto the stamp.

Dab paint onto the stamp.

2. Before you begin stamping on the project, test on a piece of scrap fabric to make sure you've applied the proper amount of paint to the stamp. Too much paint and you'll have a huge splash; too little and the design won't show.

3. When you have the right amount of paint on the stamp, stamp away.

Stamp the fabric.

 TIP

It's easy to make your own stamps by cutting designs from foam. Use Odif 303 permanent adhesive spray or other spray glue for plastic to attach the stamp to a plastic base, such as a thin piece of Styrofoam. Then glue on a fat chunk of Styrofoam for a handle.

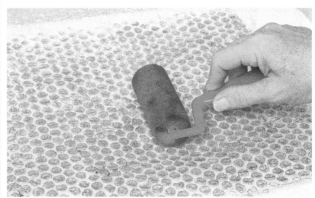

Bubble Wrap makes an interesting stamp. Here I've applied cherry paint to the Bubble Wrap with a brayer.

Lift Bubble Wrap.

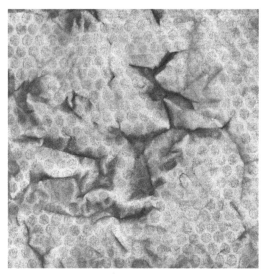

A piece of painted fabric stamped with Bubble Wrap

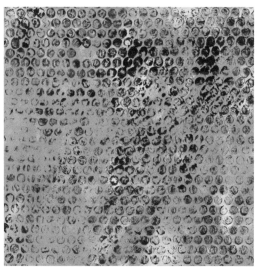

Try bold paint colors, such as black.

Soon you'll be seeing stamps everywhere! I found this seedpod on my morning walk.

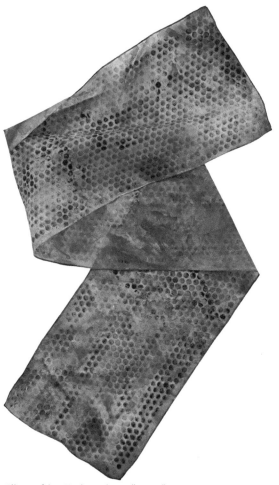

Silk scarf, by Cindy Walter, 9" × 56", 2010

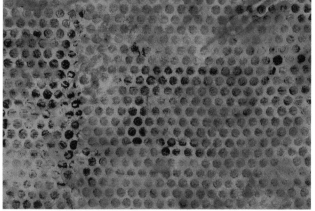

This detail of the silk scarf shows how it was painted with a color-wash and then stamped with Bubble Wrap. Remember to let any base colors dry before applying the stamp.

Stenciling

Stenciling is a perfect way to transfer sharp, clean designs to cloth. Use it to decorate your home or your quilts. In addition to opaque paints, oil-based paintsticks work beautifully with stencils.

- Any size and type of fabric, white or colored

- Stencil

- Opaque or metallic acrylic paint or Shiva Paintstiks

- Stencil brush

- Masking tape, Odif 404 Spray and Fix repositionable spray adhesive, or spray stencil adhesive (*optional*)

- Palette or plate

Suggested paints

- Liquitex Soft Body Acrylic

- Jacquard Textile or Lumiere

- Pebeo Setacolor Opaque

- Shiva Paintstiks

Directions

Refer to Basic Steps for All Projects (page 17).

notes

I like to use Shiva Paintstiks for stenciling. After applying, let dry for a few days to cure before ironing.

Work on dry fabric.

Experiment by mixing several colors in each stencil area.

1. Position the stencil on top of the fabric. Firmly hold it on the fabric with your hand or secure it with masking tape, 404 Spray and Fix, or some other type of repositionable spray stencil adhesive.

2. Pour about a teaspoon of each paint color on the palette. If you are using paintsticks, peel off the hard self-sealing cover by twisting the tip in a paper towel. Paint about a quarter-size amount of paintstick on the plate or palette.

3. Dip the stencil applicator in the paint or paintstick. Test the applicator on a paper towel or scrap fabric before painting on your actual project.

4. Lightly paint the stencil area either by pouncing up and down or using a tiny circular motion. Avoid long strokes, as this may push the paint under the stencil. Use very light pressure at first, slowly increasing the pressure until you get the desired shade of color.

Apply the paint with a pouncing or tiny circular motion.

5. Slowly lift the stencil from one corner.

Slowly remove the stencil.

6. Make sure the back of the stencil is clean before repositioning.

7. Remove oil paint from your stencil brush or sponge brush using soap and very hot water or a little turpentine. To clean your stencil, use an abrasive cleaner, such as Comet, and a sponge.

8. If you are using paintsticks, allow the paint to dry at least 24 hours. Then heat set by ironing, using a protective pressing cloth.

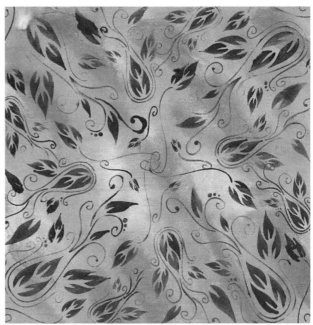

Fabric using a Windsong stencil from Embellishment Village (see Resources, page 78). The black paint adds a striking design to a dry piece of prepainted fabric.

Stencils can take on different appearances. Here, the same flower stencil that was used on the previous project (page 59) was used with green Shiva Paintstiks on prepainted spritzed fabric.

Use a light hand when stenciling on silk. Gold Jacquard Lumiere paint dresses up this red colorwash-painted scarf.

Rubbings

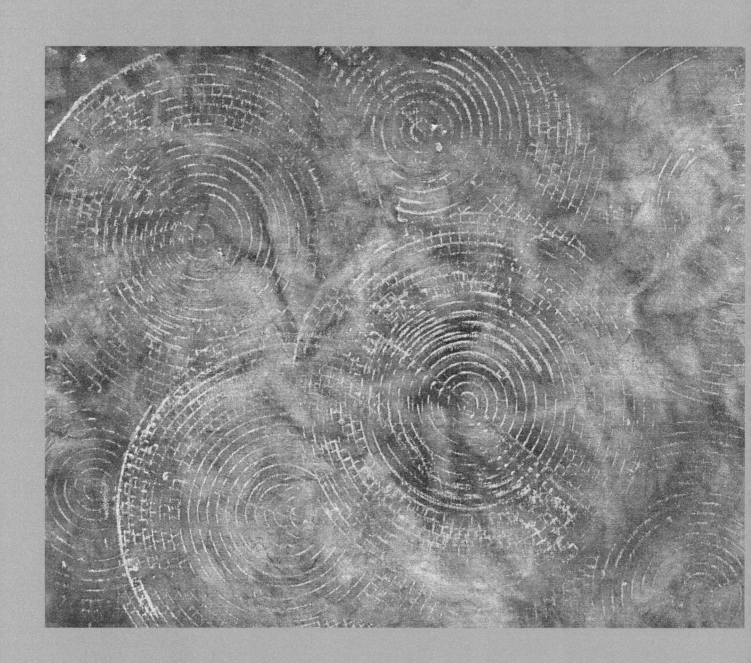

Rubbing is a fast way to add a patterned design to fabric and a great way to use the oil-based Shiva Paintstiks. This is one of my favorite techniques, because the rubbed patterns dress up any fabric. I especially like the shine of the metallic paintstiks.

SUPPLIES

- Any size and type of fabric, white or colored

- Opaque or metallic acrylic paint or Shiva Paintstiks

- Rubbing plate or items to rub, such as a plastic grid

- Stencil brush or small scraps of fabric to use as a rubbing sponge

- Palette or plate (*optional*)

Suggested paints

- Liquitex Soft Body Acrylic

- Jacquard Textile or Lumiere

- Pebeo Setacolor Opaque

- Shiva Paintstiks

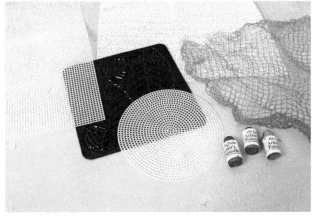

A few rubbing tools

1. Place the rubbing implement on the work surface. Place the fabric on top of the rubbing implement.

2. Rub a Shiva Paintstik, a stencil brush, or a rag with paint on it wrapped around your index finger across the fabric. Slowly increase the pressure until you have the desired results.

Directions

Refer to Basic Steps for All Projects (page 17).

- This is one of the best techniques for using Shiva Artist's Paintstiks.

- You can either buy rubbing plates or collect fun things from around your home, such as a needlepoint plastic canvas, a mesh plastic onion bag, or a large, veined leaf.

- There are several ways to apply paint when rubbing: You can rub a paintstick directly on the fabric. Or apply the paintstick or paint to a palette, and then apply to the fabric with a stencil brush. Instead of a stencil brush, I often wrap a small rag cloth around my index finger—this often works better than a brush, because it allows me to rub very lightly at first, increasing the pressure until I achieve the desired effect.

Making a rubbing: My rubbing plate is actually a needlepoint plastic canvas from a craft store.

3. To clean oil paint from your brush, use soap and very hot water or a little turpentine.

4. If you are using the oil-based paintstiks, let them dry 24 hours before ironing. Then heat set using a protective pressing cloth and an iron.

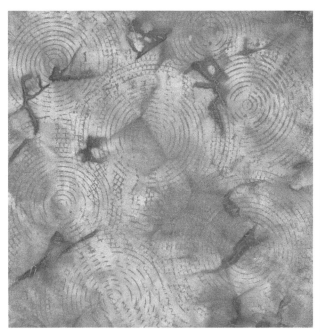

Needlepoint rubbing plate with blue oil paintstick on top of dry purple, green, and blue scrunched fabric

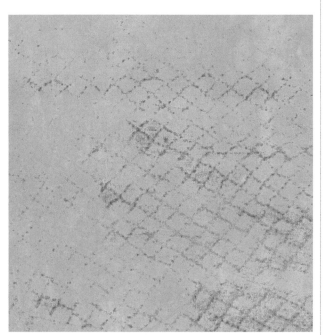

A plastic mesh produce bag was used as a rubbing plate under orange painted fabric.

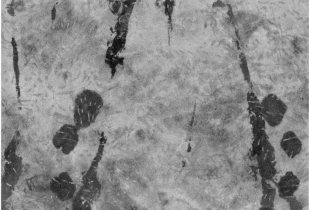

Gold metallic Shiva Paintstiks on a shibori silk scarf: The paintsticks can occasionally be too thick if rubbed right onto the fabric. Because I wanted a smooth finish on the silk, I needed to use a light hand when rubbing. I first wiped the paint onto a small cloth rag wrapped around my finger, and then I rubbed it on the silk. For this project, I used a rubbing plate from Embellishment Village (Resources, page 78).

Gallery

Lily Pond,
by Cindy Walter,
63″ × 56″, 2006

My husband's family name is Lilly, which became the inspiration for a series of lily quilts. The large background is a colorwash (page 22) of many colors. I had to work very fast to blend the colors before they dried. Once the base dried, I freehand direct painted (page 45) the water lilies and pads.

Red Anthurium,
by Elizabeth Fontanilla,
26″ × 32″, 2007

Yellow Hibiscus,
by Elizabeth Fontanilla,
26″ × 31, 2007

Elizabeth painted the background with a very light yellow wash. Once the paint was dry, she directly painted the flowers.

Bamboo on Yellow,
by Cindy Walter,
29" × 33", 2007

This quilt was made for Fairfield Processing Company when the company released its new bamboo batting in 2007. The bamboo picture is directly painted with opaque paints on a dry yellow colorwash.

Hawaiian Sunset,
by Elizabeth Fontanilla,
24″ × 30″, 2007

Elizabeth has painted most of her life. She especially likes to paint small watercolor landscapes. Here, she used opaque paints with occasional drops of water to spread the paint.

Balance,
by Cindy Walter,
10½″ × 11″, 2010

While doing a study on the balance of colors and objects, I discovered that this piece had such unique beauty that it deserved to become a quilt.

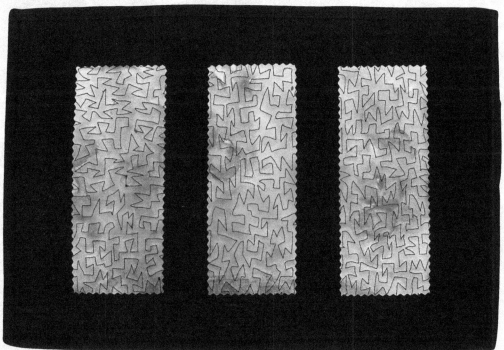

Dancing Color,
by Cindy Walter,
16″ × 10″, 2010

Colorwash panels (page 22) dance on a plain background of black fabric. The colorwash was in my reject pile. The fabrics were okay, not dazzling, but they came alive when paired with black.

Abstract Movement,
by Cindy Walter,
15" × 21", 2007

One of my favorite classes to teach on the subject of paints is wholecloth abstraction. It is directly painted on dry cloth with opaque paints. Does your brain think in swirls?

Abstract Squares,
by Cindy Walter,
17" × 21", 2008

The abstract squares are directly painted on dry cloth with opaque paints. This quilt uses the same technique as the *Abstract Movement*. Does your brain think in a square fashion?

Feathered Stars,
by Cindy Walter,
16″ × 16″, 2004

This little painted blue-and-white quilt is one of my favorites. I was planning to create a miniature feathered star quilt, when it occurred to me that it would be easier to paint it than to piece it. This is one of the first miniature painted quilts (page 41) that I created.

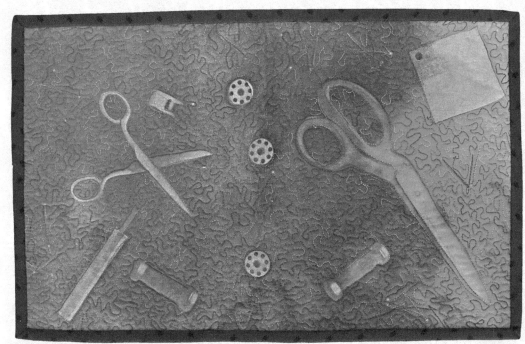

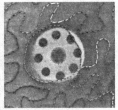

The Work Table,
by Stevii Graves,
17″ × 10½″, 2009

As a fun experiment and tribute to her art, Stevii gathered scissors, spools of thread, bobbins, and even her much used seam ripper from her studio and took them outside to create this darling heliographic quilt (page 32).

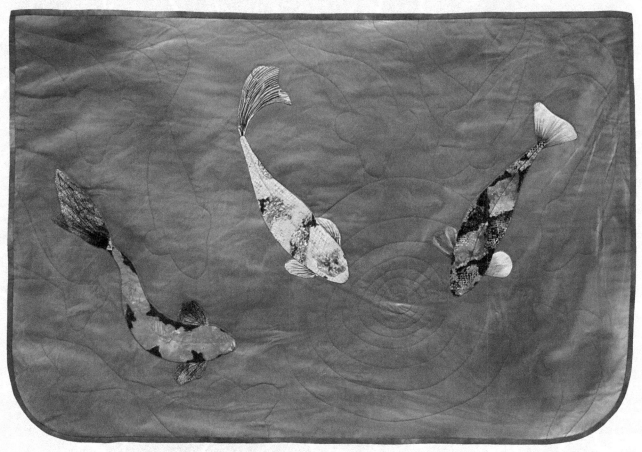

Koi Pond,
by Stevii Graves,
34″ × 25″, 2010

Stevii painted a perfect blue and green color-wash (page 22) with Liquitex Soft Body Acrylic paints as the background for her striking hand-appliquéd koi. She finished the project by quilting lines of fish and water ripples to showcase the koi.

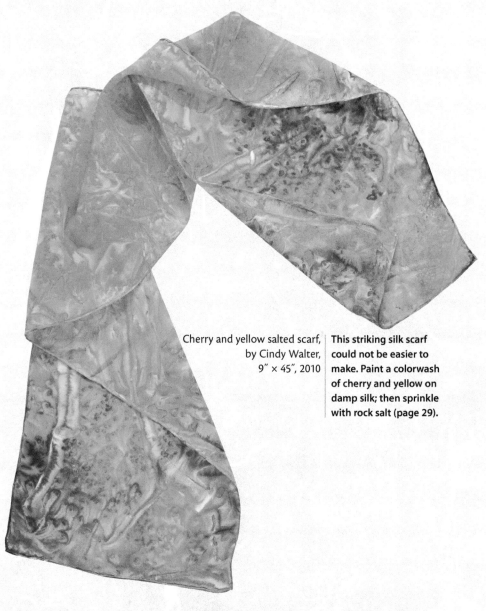

Cherry and yellow salted scarf, by Cindy Walter, 9" × 45", 2010 | This striking silk scarf could not be easier to make. Paint a colorwash of cherry and yellow on damp silk; then sprinkle with rock salt (page 29).

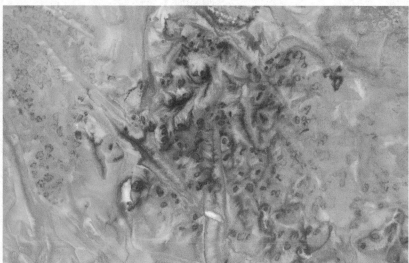

Notice how the salt makes incredible marks in the paint, creating the design for you.

Cindy doll,
by elinor peace bailey,
25″ tall, 2008

Using scraps of cotton and silk fabric that Cindy painted with Dye-na-Flow paints, elinor made this doll for a workshop on creativity that she and Cindy taught together. After attaching the blond hair, elinor couldn't resist naming the doll "Cindy." In addition to creating unique dolls, elinor also enjoys painting using Lumiere, Dye-na-Flow, and Tee Juice (a permanent ink pen). She is a great fan of painting on stabilized cotton. See more of elinor's talent and doll patterns on elinor's website at www.epbdolls.net.

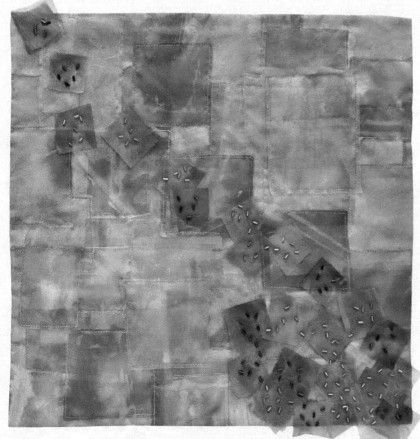

Tumbling Blocks,
by Lynn Koolish,
20″ × 20″, 2010

The fabrics for this quilt (silks and organzas) were painted colorwashes using diluted **Liquitex Soft Body Acrylic** paints in a workshop led by **Emily Richardson.**

Patterns

Miniature Dutchman's Puzzle pattern (project on page 41)

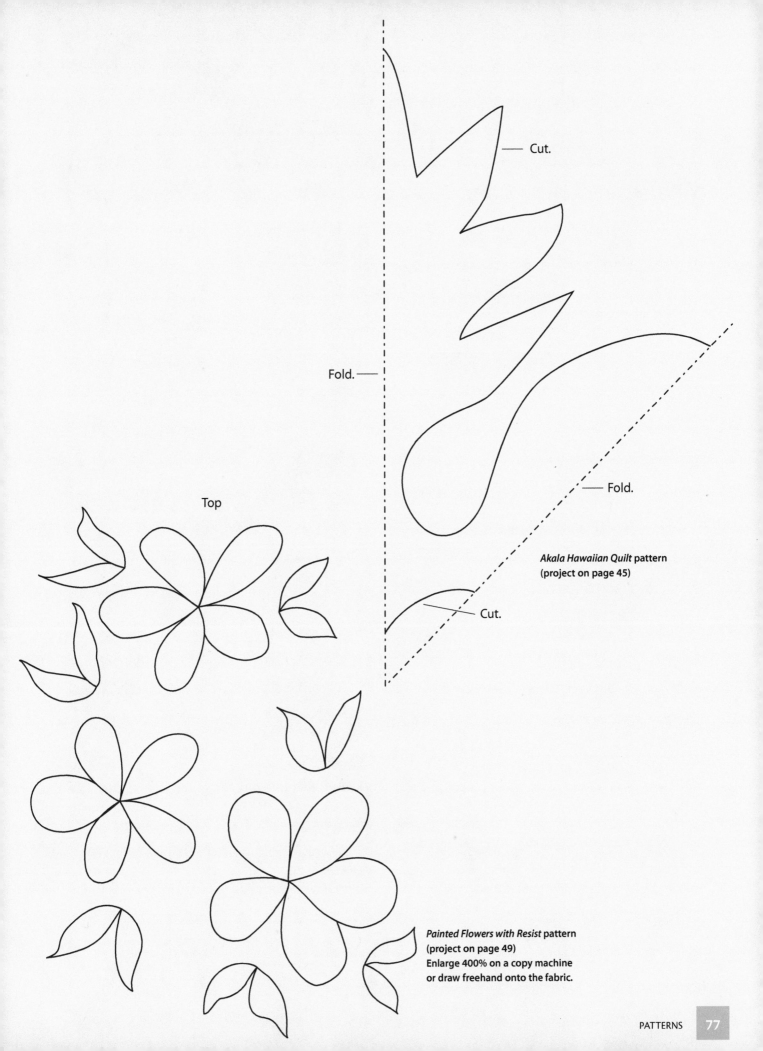

Cut.

Fold.

Fold.

Akala Hawaiian Quilt **pattern**
(project on page 45)

Cut.

Top

Painted Flowers with Resist **pattern**
(project on page 49)
Enlarge 400% on a copy machine
or draw freehand onto the fabric.

Resources

FAVORITE WEBSITES

www.cindywalter.com
Teaching information, books, and inspiration

www.ctpub.com
Books; DVDs; Liquitex Soft Body Acrylic paints, inks, and mediums; Derwent Inktense pencils; Lutradur; and more

www.jacquardproducts.com
Wholesale only paints, dyes, resist, and Cindy Walter's Stabilized Cotton. Full of inspiration, patterns, and tips.

www.artisticartifacts.com
Stewart Gill and Shiva Paintstiks

www.dharmatrading.com
All types of paints, dyes, and clothing to paint

www.dickblick.com
Basic art supplies, including gutta

www.embellishmentvillage.com
Shiva Paintstiks, stencils, and much more

www.joggles.com
Basic craft supplies, paints, and embellishments

www.jwdpublishing.com
Quilting and sewing patterns

www.myneedlesandnotions.com
Cindy Walter's Stabilized Cotton and hard-to-find hand needles

www.prochemicalanddye.com
Paints, Shiva Paintstiks, and stencils

www.quilterstv.com
Free public network for quilters

www.quiltingarts.com
Great inspiration, teaching, and magazine

SUGGESTED READING AND VIEWING

Art Cloth, Jane Dunnewold, Interweave Press, 2010

Creative Mixed Media, Sherrill Kahn, Martingale & Co., 2010

Create Your Own Hand-Printed Cloth, Rayna Gillman, C&T Publishing, 2008

Jane Davila's Surface Design Essentials, Jane Davila, C&T Publishing, 2010

Luminous Landscapes, Gloria Loughman, C&T Publishing, 2007

Mickey Lawler Teaches You to Paint Landscape Fabric (DVD), Mickey Lawler, C&T Publishing, 2010

Mickey Lawler's SkyQuilts, Mickey Lawler, C&T Publishing, Inc., 2011

Off-the-Shelf Fabric Painting, Sue Beevers, C&T Publishing, 2004

Shibori: The Art of Fabric Tying, Folding, Pleating, and Dyeing, Elfriede Möller, Search Press, 1999

Shibori Designs & Techniques, Mandy Southan, Search Press, 2009

Shibori for Textile Artists, Janice Gunner, Kodansha America, 2010

Skydyes, Mickey Lawler, C&T Publishing, 1999

The Surface Designer's Handbook, Holly Brackmann, Interweave Press, 2006

About the Author

Photo by Mark Anderson

Cindy is an author, television host, and teacher of traditional and contemporary quilt techniques. She has been interested in quilting since childhood, having been taught by her grandmother while growing up in the farm country of Iowa. In 1996, her first book, *Snippet Sensations*, won the Primedia Award of Excellence. The craze of her Snippet technique made the book an international best seller and opened the door for Cindy to teach the art of quilting around the world. She has had wonderful adventures and has great fondness for her students throughout the United States, Europe, New Zealand, Australia, and Japan. This is her tenth book.

In addition to appearing on eight different quilting television shows, Cindy was cohost of the PBS TV show *Quilt Central*. You can still catch her on TV and the web, hosting for www.quilterstv.com, where she is the network's full-time interviewer.

Cindy resides in Oahu, Hawaii, with her husband, Michael A. Lilly, a practicing attorney and former state Attorney General, and their teenage son, Alex, and two cats. For leisure, Cindy and Michael enjoy swimming, reading at their north shore beach home, and hiking. In addition to hiking around the United States, they have traveled overseas to hike in Spain, Portugal, England, Scotland, Norway, Australia, New Zealand, France, Austria, Switzerland, Germany, Italy, and Croatia.

Cindy Walter may be reached at cindyquilter@aol.com.

Great Titles and Products *from* C&T PUBLISHING

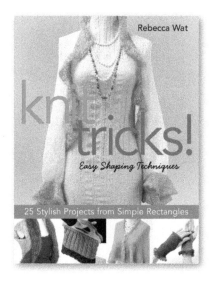

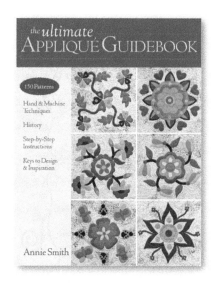

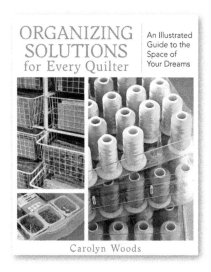

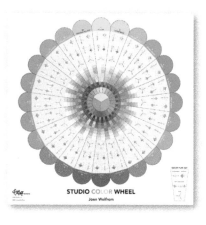

Available at your local retailer or **www.ctpub.com** *or* **800-284-1114**

For a list of other fine books from C&T Publishing, visit our website to view our catalog online.

C&T PUBLISHING, INC.

P.O. Box 1456
Lafayette, CA 94549
800-284-1114

Email: ctinfo@ctpub.com
Website: www.ctpub.com

C&T Publishing's professional photography services are now available to the public. Visit us at www.ctmediaservices.com.

Tips and Techniques *can be found at www.ctpub.com > Consumer Resources > Quiltmaking Basics: Tips & Techniques for Quiltmaking & More*

For quilting supplies:

COTTON PATCH

1025 Brown Ave.
Lafayette, CA 94549
Store: 925-284-1177
Mail order: 925-283-7883

Email: CottonPa@aol.com
Website: www.quiltusa.com

Note: Fabrics used in the quilts shown may not be currently available, as fabric manufacturers keep most fabrics in print for only a short time.